Elevate your e
and wonder

Advent at Waverley Abbey Trust

- Advent retreats for reflection and inspiration

- Devotional material, drawing you into deeper exploration of the season

- Advent themed evenings at Waverley Abbey House

- Books and online resources

To find out more visit
waverleyabbeyresources.org/advent

Inner **peace**

John 14:25–27

'Do not let your hearts be troubled, and do not let them be afraid.' (v27, NRSVA)

My spiritual health is enhanced when I experience inner peace. Inner peace doesn't come easily to me. As you may well have heard a preacher say, there is one 'fear not' in the Bible for every day of the year. If you feel fear, then very clearly you are not alone.

'Peace I leave with you; my peace I give you. I do not give to you as the world gives' (v27), says Jesus to His disciples as He promises the Holy Spirit. The peace that the Holy Spirit offers, another fruit, is again something that we can experience despite our circumstances. That's why it is different to that of the world. My spiritual health flourishes when I am at peace. That is when I am trusting God, believing that there can be a redemptive outcome to challenging things that happen. It is when I believe that God will guide me and lead me into places where I can flourish, and believe that I am fulfilling my calling and vocation. Sometimes that needs a bit of reframing, acknowledging that there are lots of little daily choices, faithful actions – what feels like mundane routine but which is about being who others may need us to be in order for them to be spiritually healthy too.

One of the ways I look to find inner peace is through rooting myself at the beginning of the day with God. I can commit the day to God, journal about things which may be troubling me from the previous day or day ahead, read the Bible, pray and just be quiet in God's presence. If I start the day with inner peace then I am carrying something helpful with me through the day, and can go back in my head to that sense of peace I started the day with.

For prayer and reflection

Thank You, God, for giving us the peace that passes all understanding and for helping us to fear not. Amen.

Inspiring
Women
Every Day

November

SPIRITUAL HEALTH M.O.T.

SALLY NASH

December

EXPECTATION AND WONDER

ROSALYN DERGES

MIX
Paper from
responsible sources
FSC® C021017
www.fsc.org

WAVERLEY ABBEY
RESOURCES
OPERATING NAME OF **CWR**

Sally Nash

(Revd Dr) Sally Nash is a freelance theological educator, researcher, mentor and spiritual accompanier. She is an associate minister, Senior Research Fellow and a researcher with a chaplaincy team. She has worked in Christian Ministry for 35+ years training people for ministry particularly work with children and young people. Sally enjoys walking, drinking good coffee and eating dark chocolate and blogging!

Rosalyn Derges

Rosalyn has been involved with Waverley Abbey Trust for 20 years, teaching on a counselling course, serving with the Inspiring Women's ministry team on courses and weekends as well as writing for IWED. She enjoys walking by the sea, discovering the best coffee shops, and comparing good fish and chips!

Spiritual Health M.O.T

SALLY NASH

I try to give as much attention to my spiritual wellbeing as I do my physical and mental wellbeing. That's why spiritual health is so important to me. Over the next four weeks, I will share with you the four different dimensions of spiritual health that I focus on: our relationships with self, others, God and nature/environment. The Bible has so much to say about each of these areas and we will explore how we can enhance our spiritual health through applying biblical wisdom.

I make no apologies for starting with such a familiar verse; it is one I have recited to myself for over 50 years which means the King James Version runs through my head. I prefer this version's use of 'everlasting' rather than 'eternal' life. In a culture of things that do not last long, of quick fixes, of impermanence, that my life with God is everlasting gives me a sense that I have invested wisely in my choice to follow Jesus.

My starting premise is that we have security in who we are through our faith in Jesus, the promise of eternal life and God's love for us. My relationship with myself starts with recognising that security, and returning to it on those days when I look in the mirror and see reflected back my insecurities, anxieties or weariness – or one of the myriad of other feelings I might experience. I have been on a journey in my relationship with myself, growing in appreciation of the Sally that God created as I have got to know her better and see her flourish as she pays attention to her spiritual health and wellbeing and the relationships that contribute to that.

John 3:16–18

'He gave his only begotten Son, that whosoever believeth in him [should]… have everlasting life.'
(v16, KJV)

For prayer and reflection

Thank You, God, that our spiritual health flows out of the security we have in You, Your love and Your promise of eternal life. Amen.

Identity

The question 'who am I?' is one of the most profound that we can ever ask. It can take a long time to answer as we try out different selves or take on different identities over the years. Sometimes our identity becomes wrapped up in a role – a child, a parent, a mechanic, a teacher, a footballer, a singer – there are so many different roles we inhabit. Our relationship with our self, our self-esteem and self-perception, is sometimes caught up in the value we and others see in these roles.

Each time I get distracted from seeing myself as anything beyond a precious child of God, I come back to these verses. My spiritual health cannot be dependent on what I do; otherwise what happens when I can no longer do it or the role is taken from me? My relationship with myself is best not based on my qualifications or my accomplishments, as there will be days to come when they will mean nothing to who I am in that moment.

The Northumbria Community, of which I am a part, encourages us to say the Methodist Covenant Prayer which includes the lines: 'put me to what you will, rank me with whom you will; put me to doing, put me to suffering; let me be employed for you, or laid aside for you, exalted for you or brought low for you'*. I find these words so challenging and struggle to say them sometimes, but they remind me that my identity is rooted in who I am in God, and in nothing else. I am God's precious child. On the days when I find that hard to appropriate, I sometimes find that gazing on a picture of Jesus helps me connect with the reality of that preciousness and stripped-back identity.

For prayer and reflection

Loving God, thank You that we are Your precious children, and that our identity is not to be found in external things but in You. Amen.

* methodist.org.uk/about-us/the-methodist-church/what-is-distinctive-about-methodism/a-covenant-with-god/

Self-awareness

'If I must boast, I will boast of the things that show my weakness.'
(v30)

I
f I asked you to pick five words which best describe you, which five would you choose? I wonder which the apostle Paul would have chosen? Courageous? Passionate? Impulsive? Self-awareness is important in our spiritual health. It helps us explore our calling and live out our Christian life.

I agree with Paul that we need to be aware that we are weak and need to depend on God. But we also have gifts, strengths, qualities that God gives us. Understanding where we are weak, where we might be vulnerable, helps us make wise choices.

When you read Paul's letters you might think that they should come with a trigger warning – follow Jesus and here is a long list of difficult things which might happen to you. Not many of us end up literally shipwrecked these days, but we might find ourselves metaphorically shipwrecked and then our weaknesses may seem very apparent. But how often do we learn so much about ourselves that when things go wrong? John Calvin argued in his *Institutes of the Christian Religion* that 'Nearly all wisdom we possess, that is to say, true and sound wisdom, consists of two parts: the knowledge of God and of ourselves'*.

I know that one of my weaknesses is that I find it hard to talk about death, but one of my roles is as a parish priest so I cannot then say I will just avoid that. I know when I am doing a pastoral visit or talking to someone that I can draw on God's strength in me, the guidance of the Holy Spirit, to be able to engage as I need to and as God calls me to in that role. Weakness makes me a better minister in this area.

reformed.org/books/institutes/books/book1/bk1ch01.html

For prayer and reflection

Thank You, God, that in our weaknesses we can draw on Your strength; help us depend on You. Amen.

Fullness of **joy**

Psalm 16:5–11

'You show me the path of life. In your presence there is fullness of joy' (v11, NRSVA)

I s there anyone else reading this and singing, 'Joy is a flag flying high in the castle of my heart'? Maybe not, but joy is a fruit of the Spirit (Gal. 5:22) that I particularly prize. While I might ask God to give me whichever fruit I need for the challenges of the day ahead, joy is what perhaps makes the biggest difference to my spiritual health.

Joy is not the same as happiness. Happiness tends to be based on external circumstances: I am not happy when my team loses another match; I am not happy when I see a rat running through my garden. Yet I usually have a deep sense of joy and it comes out of my relationship with God.

The psalmist in our reading today talks about the Lord being our chosen lot. I had both a crisis and a process conversion. I got to know God over my childhood through Sunday School and other activities, but I responded to a call to give my life to God as a teenager in a Baptist Church. I chose God. I chose a God who is with me, who guides me, leads me, gives me wisdom, but most of all gives me fullness of joy. I have learnt that the joy bubbles in me whatever is happening in my external world. I might be facing very challenging circumstances, but I know, from experiences over the years, that God is with me in them, regardless of whether or not I have a sense of God's presence. That leaves me with a remnant of joy, which most days is a fullness of joy as I celebrate another day to serve God. If you are struggling to find the path or to sense the joy, then pray and perhaps ask God whom you should speak to about this. Sometimes we need God in human form to help us.

For prayer and reflection

Gracious God, thank You for the fullness of joy that we find in Your presence and for Your guidance day by day. Amen.

Weekend

Labour of love

....

1 Thessalonians 1:1–10

'Remembering before our God and Father your work of faith and labour of love' (v3, NRSVA)

'Labour of love' is such an evocative phrase and reminds me of the many people who make ministry possible in our churches and Christian organisations. Most of us will have been in a shop or restaurant and been served by someone who is a little grumpy or sharp with us. That's not a good experience. As we serve God, let's remember that it is a labour of love and do it with a loving attitude and heart.

What we do has meaning and while it may not be talked about in the way that Paul talks about the church at Thessalonica in our passage today, what we do will be noticed and discussed. Our spiritual health is enhanced if we have a sense of meaning, and sometimes that sense of meaning can be helpfully understood within a corporate context, not just as an individual. Thus, our labours of love are often done within a team and we can cheer each other on and encourage that service. Being together can bring an added dimension to our labours. What stories might others tell about your labours of love?

....

Optional further reading

Peter Scazzero, *Emotionally Healthy Spirituality* (Nashville, TN: Thomas Nelson, 2006)

Our relationship with **others**

Luke 10:38–42

'Martha, Martha, you are worried and distracted by many things' (v41)

Are you a Martha or a Mary? In this passage, we see Martha very frustrated with Mary who isn't helping her as she thinks she should. One of the things which took me too many years to learn was not to compare myself to others. I tended not to complain like Martha does in this passage, at least not out loud; but resenting other people is so damaging to our spiritual health.

I wonder whether Mary and Martha ever had a conversation about this incident? Did they agree to disagree or did they see each other's perspectives. Hospitality was such a core value that what Martha was doing was being a good host and providing for her guests. Mary was learning – she was being a disciple, sitting at the feet of Jesus. Another good thing to do.

Sometimes we have to choose between two things which are good, and we need to make the choice for ourselves. In a contemporary context, perhaps Martha would have ordered take-out food and then would have been able to listen along with Mary.

Perhaps, too, it would be helpful to reflect on whether there are areas of life where we feel a bit like Martha, a little put-upon maybe, perhaps resentful for a lack of appreciation? Are there people we need to talk with to explore some of our roles or expectations on this? My husband and I eventually found a great way of dividing up the household chores which works for both of us, but not before both of us had been frustrated with the other. If you are wondering what that was, I do the time-significant tasks, Paul those which can be done anytime. I am a bit of both Mary and Martha – hopefully the good parts!

For prayer and reflection

Help us, God, not to compare ourselves to others, and to focus on being Your disciple. Amen.

Known by our **love**

John 13:33–35

'By this everyone will know that you are my disciples, if you have love for one another' (v35)

This is one of the most challenging passages in the whole of the New Testament. Jesus is giving us a new commandment and it can be harder to keep than the original ten. Loving others isn't always easy but it is what Jesus asks us to do.

One of my previous jobs involved looking after gap-year teams. Over thirty years on, I can still remember the words of one church leader about a team based in a really tough area. He commented that the church had had learnt more from observing the relationships the team members had with one another than anything they had done. The team had not seen it in themselves and were so encouraged to hear this. It was this verse in action.

Did you ever play with daisies when you were a child – pulling off the petals and saying, 'loves me, loves me not'. For my first sermon after I was ordained, I found a picture of a daisy with only one petal and the caption was, 'Start with God loves you'. As we love others, we start with knowing that God loves us and realising the importance of loving ourselves.

So, in our relationship with others how can we be known for our love? Think of one relationship you have that you find a little challenging: what is something loving you can do towards that person? It may be to send them a card appreciating something about them, or taking some flowers or fruit from your garden or a cake you have made.

I rarely think of love as a feeling; it is more of an act of will. If I only acted lovingly when I felt loving, that could be tricky! So don't depend on feelings. Think about actions and attitudes in your relationship with others instead.

For prayer and reflection

Loving God, thank You for the love that You pour out on us. Help us to share it with one another. Amen.

Hospitality

....

Romans 12:9–13

....

'Contribute to the
needs of the saints;
extend hospitality
to strangers.' (v13)

Hospitality was core to both my husband and I becoming disciples of Jesus. As young Christians and then new to churches (before we knew each other), it was being invited into people's houses and eating with them that helped us understand so much more of what it meant to be a disciple, not just a Christian. In both our cases, hospitality was extended when we were little more than strangers to our hosts.

My spiritual health is enhanced by being with people who love, accept and affirm me, and this is often more possible in smaller gatherings in people's homes. One of the huge losses of lockdown has been not being able to gather in those safe places where we can build one another up.

However, hospitality is not just about being with people we know and like but involves extending the invitation to those who we might not know, who may be on the fringes or margins, who might be on their own. Church which is cliquey isn't really church as it should be. Working at including all who want to belong, and helping them feel they do belong, is what the essence of good hospitality should be about.

One of the most important roles in a local church belongs to those who greet you as you arrive. It makes such a difference to be welcomed in by someone who is genuine in that welcome.

We can also think about how we do hospitality when it isn't practical at home. Are there local cafés or places to gather where we can be on more neutral ground? Not everyone finds it easy to go to someone else's home. Look to be hospitable in a way which fits with the culture of where you are.

....

**For prayer
and reflection**

....

**We thank You, God,
for the hospitality
we have been
offered. Help us to
welcome the
stranger into our
midst. Amen.**

Second chances

Acts 15:36–40

'Barnabas wanted to take John, also called Mark, with them' (v37)

A re you a 'three strikes and they are out' type of person when it comes to disagreements? This passage is one that makes me feel sad, although I know the whole backstory of such decisions is never heard. Paul and Barnabas go their separate ways because they cannot agree about taking John Mark with them. Barnabas, the encourager, wants to give him another chance. Paul doesn't.

In our relationships with others, how do we view second chances? Or third? Or fourth? How many of us are where we are today because someone took a risk on us and gave us a second chance? Sometimes, we might be so badly hurt that a second chance would be detrimental to our own wellbeing; I am not talking about giving second chances in those sorts of circumstances. But how grateful would John Mark have been to Barnabas who looked past his mistakes and trusted him to be different this time?

In the past I worked with young people who presented with challenging behaviours at times. When you knew some of the things that had happened in their lives, it was clear why they might have struggled to trust me. They needed to test me out, to see if I was who I said I was, to see if I would stick around and not abandon them like others had in the past. We might meet people in our church settings who struggle to trust, who have been let down by others, who may come to us after being rejected elsewhere. For their spiritual health, they need people who will accept them, welcome them, value them. Who might need a second chance in your context at the moment? Can you give them one? Do *you* need a second chance?

For prayer and reflection

Thank You, God, that You always give us another chance, that You are always our encourager. Amen.

Encouragement

**Hebrews
10:23–25**

'And let us consider
how we may spur
one another on
towards love and
good deeds' (v24)

I love random acts of kindness. I can still vividly picture the woman in the queue at the supermarket who gave me a bar of fair trade chocolate. It was so encouraging, I felt blessed and my spirits were lifted. Random acts of kindness are often something I take up as an activity in Lent and then try to do one a week afterwards. The woman's act of kindness to me provoked me to good deeds. If this is not part of your usual practice, why not try one in the next week?

The verses we are reading today are talking about encouraging within the body of believers, and are part of a wider paragraph on persevering. I love the encouragers that I meet, those people who help me see myself in a positive light, who affirm me, who can see things that perhaps I only see a little dimly. Who are those people that encourage you? What can you learn from them? Who do you know that needs encouraging at the moment? What can you do to encourage them? As someone who has been a leader for very many years, I know that sometimes people find it hard to encourage their leaders for a lot of different reasons. You might also think about how you encourage on social media if you use it. It can be a good way to encourage publicly and perhaps model the practice for others.

I am most blessed by encouragement that is about who I am rather than what I do, although it is always good to hear that someone enjoyed my book or reflection. It also helps me to understand that I am loved for who I am not what I do, as there will be times when I can no longer do what I once did.

**For prayer
and reflection**

**Gracious God, help
us to be
encouragers, to
spur one another
on to love and
good deeds. Amen.**

Weekend

Kindness

....

Luke 10:25–37

'Which of these three do you think was a neighbour' (v36)

T his story, usually knows as that of the Good Samaritan, is one I can listen to time and time again. The unexpected person showed kindness, they saw a person in need and did what they could to meet that need. The people in the story we might have expected to be helpful walked past on the other side.

We live in times where there is significant cultural conflict, where there is prejudice, stereotyping, discrimination and behaviour which is not kind or loving. At my church, we have been listening to the stories of our BAME congregation members. I have been brought to tears as they have told of how unwelcoming people in their neighbourhoods have been and sadly, for some of them, how church didn't welcome them either.

The good Samaritan in the story confounds stereotypes, acts with compassion and kindness, and does what we hope someone would do for us if we lay injured on the ground – he goes to help.

I wonder how we can reach out across boundaries and barriers and show kindness in the way that Jesus encourages in this story? Everyone is our neighbour.

....

Optional further reading

Fiona Stratta, *Walking with Biblical Women of Courage* (Abingdon: BRF, 2017).

Our **relationship** with God

Joshua 24:24–27

'We will serve the
LORD our God
and obey him'
(v24)

This verse comes at the end of the story of Joshua, who I imagine died happy in the knowledge that those he led had chosen to serve God. I can still remember a conversation I had with God in my early twenties when, after a bit of a rocky time, I felt God saying to me that I needed to make a decision – was I going to wholeheartedly serve Him? He gave me a choice and I said yes.

That decision changed my life. Ever since then, that question of whom I am serving is at the front of my thoughts as I explore vocation, decisions and lifestyle. Now, I am not saying that I always get it right but my intention is to serve God. I believe God has given me passions and that in following these passions I am serving God. One of those passions is equipping the saints for works of service (Eph. 4:12). What are your passions? How are you using those to serve God?

The topsy-turvy thing about our service, though, is that God in Jesus came to earth to serve (Matt. 20:28). We learn best how to serve by following the example of Jesus who talks about doing what He sees the Father doing. So where are you seeing God at work? This is often known as 'missio Dei', seeing what God is doing and joining in. That can mean we end up serving in unexpected places as we see God at work. So many have been doing great work through lockdown, serving alongside neighbours in food banks, for example. We serve God in the everyday, in the places where He sends us, to the people He sends us to. Where and who is that for you? It might be that you do this without even leaving home. Despite our circumstances, God calls us to serve.

**For prayer
and reflection**

**Thank You, God,
for the blessing
and privilege it is
to serve You and to
know You are our
Servant King.
Amen.**

Worship

Psalm 84

'How lovely is your dwelling-place' (v1)

Where do you enjoy worshipping God? In church with music? On your own in private? Out for a walk in nature? Or all of these and more? Worship is giving glory and honour to the God who created and saved us.

While worship is more than singing, there is something special about that activity; the music and words combined communicate deeply. I was talking to a friend about how much joy she finds in leading the singing of hymns in the home for people with dementia she works in. The music and the words often trigger memories, and they sing along with joy. I have hymns and songs which particularly lift my spirits and which I sing, sometimes in my head, sometimes out loud. One of those is *Great is Thy Faithfulness*, which encourages me to look back and see the journey I have been on with God and how I can trust in God's faithfulness even at those times when I can't quite see the next step in the journey. Music and singing can lift our spirits and sometimes reaches us in a way that other things do not.

Today's reading is a psalm, so many of which invite us to worship God. Psalm 84 encourages us to dwell with God. While I believe I can meet with God anywhere, I have a special place at home where I spend time with God first thing, a routine which I find helps me start the day with worship.

I also try to visit what some call 'thin places', those places where God seems closer. Often these are locations where, for many, many years, people have worshipped God and prayed. They are a place of pilgrimage, where saints have gone to worship and encounter God. They enhance my spiritual health.

For prayer and reflection

Thank You, God, for the freedom to worship You. Help us to find joy and peace as we fix our eyes on You. Amen.

Made in God's **image**

Genesis 1:25–27

'In the image of God he created them; male and female he created them.' (v27)

Each time I look at someone, I try to remember that they are made in the image of God, the doctrine known as 'imago Dei'. Being made in God's image is about who we are and not what we do. God loves us for who we are, God's precious children, not for what we accomplish in God's name. Unconditional love for who we are is quite rare, but we are God's beloved and living in the truth of that can be challenging and take time to be fully grounded in our lives.

It also needs to be lived out in our relationships with others. How we treat other people reflects our view of God and what it means to be human. This means we need to be mindful of how we treat everyone we come into contact with. One of the ways we can assess the quality of our relationship with God is how we treat other children of God.

A story which really brings this home to me is that of Zacchaeus in Luke 19:1–10. Jesus spots Zacchaeus up a tree and asks if He can go to his house. Jesus, the Son of God, spots a despised tax collector and expresses a desire to go and be with him. Jesus looked beyond the surface and encountered someone He knew to be made in God's image and whom He invited into a relationship with Him. There are many stories through the Gospels where Jesus reaches out to people who others despised or rejected. Jesus' encounter with the woman at the well (John 4:1–42) is another one; even His disciples were surprised to see them talking together. We may want to consider how we reach out beyond cultural and other barriers, following the example of Jesus.

For prayer and reflection

Loving God, we thank You that all of us are made in Your image. Help us to know we are Your beloved. Amen.

Keeping on...

'Keep on doing the things that you have learned' (v9, NRSVA)

What have you been learning from God recently? Reading Bible notes is a great way to keep on learning, but learning often needs implementing. The letter to the Philippians is encouraging the church to keep on doing the things that they have been learning about. This passage is a great summary of some of those things which we can always keep on doing! They are fundamental to our life as a Christian.

We are twice told to rejoice, in this passage, so this seems to be particularly important. I remember singing this verse as a round when I was a teenager. It embedded the idea in my heart and mind that rejoicing was a good thing to do. Each day there is some dimension of God we can rejoice in, something we are grateful for, a quality of God we particularly appreciate that day.

We are also encouraged to be gentle. Gentleness is sometimes an underrated quality, but so needed. It can take discipline to respond with gentleness but, as we know, being gentle will often get a better response from someone.

I have written about not worrying earlier in the month, but many of us need regular reminders of this. One of the reasons I love my bird feeders is that they remind me of Jesus' words in Matthew 6:26; if I care for the birds in my garden, how much more does God care about me?

What we think about impacts us. This passage gives us a list of beneficial things we can think about. We might do that by subscribing to a helpful regular email, follow someone on social media who posts encouraging sayings or pictures, have a book which we dip into that inspires us. What might you plan to keep on doing?

For prayer and reflection

Thank You, God, for all we are learning about You. Help us to put this learning into action. Amen.

....

....

'those who wait for the LORD shall renew their strength' (v31)

Renewing our strength

Our energy ebbs and flows. While that is clear with physical energy it may also be true of our emotional energy. I know that when I am physically tired this impacts my emotions, and sometimes my spiritual energy too.

This passage is one of my go-to places when I feel like this. It reminds me of the importance of stilling myself, resting and having time out to begin to feel restored and renew my energy. There have been times, like following major surgery, where the wait to renew my strength has been long; and I know some people find their strength diminished over many months, or even years. Those are such challenging times, when waiting can be so painful, when we don't understand. Our relationship with God can be confusing when life is difficult or challenging. I have learnt that my body does not always function as I hope it might and that none of us has perfect bodies, and that although I believe God does do miracles (and have seen and heard about them) it is rare for God to work outside of the way our bodies usually work. So sometimes renewing our strength will be about holding on, and sometimes just holding on.

Not understanding is one of the biggest challenges we face as Christians and it is at those times that we particularly need to trust in the character of God, and to remind ourselves of God's love for us. These times are not easy and finding the best ways to wait and be renewed is something each one of us needs to work out for ourselves – sometimes with the help and support of a spiritual accompanier, our church minister or a good friend who stands with us as we wait.

....

For prayer and reflection

....

Gracious God, help us as we wait for our strength to be renewed, that we might soar again. Amen.

Weekend

Being restored

....

John 21:15–19

'Lord, you know everything; you know that I love you.' (v17)

I can identify with Peter and imagine how he would have felt shame having denied Jesus (Luke 22:54–62) when he said he would never do that. I love this story of breakfast on the beach. If I could put myself in only one story from the Bible, this would be it. Breakfast out is always a treat for me, but imagine having my breakfast cooked by Jesus. And on a beach – where better?

This story gives me hope, that when I blow it, when I get something wrong, there is a way back. That I am not lost forever, but that, in Jesus, I have a Saviour who forgives and restores. In this story, Jesus asks Peter three times, 'do you love me'. If it were me I would be getting a bit irritated by the third time, but the echoes of those three denials would have come to mind as I realised how gracious Jesus was in restoring the commission He had given me previously.

As I think about my spiritual health, knowing that I am living out my calling is significant. It can help me frame some of the things I might find more challenging in a positive way, knowing that this is part of my ongoing journey with God.

....

Optional further reading

Margaret Silf, *Landmarks, An Ignatian journey* (London: DLT, 1998)

Our relationship with **nature**

Psalm 19:1–6

'The heavens declare the glory of God' (v1)

I love to watch the sky, both day and night. The colours, the clouds, the sun, the stars, the moon. All of these things give me a sense of awe and a desire to praise God. Obviously, some days and places offer more beauty but the ever-changing scenes remind me of our creator God.

I can still remember the first time I really saw stars. I had finally arrived somewhere without street lights, far from the light pollution they cause. I could not believe how many stars there were in the sky, and as my eyes became accustomed to the darkness I began to see more and more – beautiful.

The psalmist is clear that, despite the lack of words, no audible voice, there are words that go out to the ends of the earth from seeing the beauty of the heavens. I wonder what words you 'hear' as you look out? At this time of year we are usually awake for both sunrise and sunset. Where I live, there will be just over eight hours of daylight today. I could time my walk in the park for either sunrise or sunset, or the moon in the evening. And as I walk or look, I can reflect on the greatness of God and the faithfulness of the sun, moon and stars which appear just as expected, and which help me understand how God is faithful. As the hymn says, 'morning by morning new mercies I see'.*

One of my most precious memories is associated with nature. For a special birthday we went to Lapland because I wanted to see the Northern Lights, the aurora borealis. The magic of the green dancing lights across the intensely dark sky was breathtaking. The heavens that night really did declare the glory of God to me.

For prayer and reflection

Thank You, God, for the beauty of nature, for the way that You speak to us through it. Amen.

*Great is Thy Faithfulness, lyrics by Thomas Obediah Chisholm; music by William Marion Runyan (Carol Stream, IL: Hope Publishing, 1923)

Seeing **rainbows**

Genesis 9:8–17

'Whenever the rainbow appears in the clouds, I will see it and remember the everlasting covenant' (v16)

Rainbows are a sign of hope for me. Rainbows have appeared in the sky at significant times of loss, and it felt as if God was saying that I could still trust, I could still have hope, despite my lack of understanding at the time about what had happened. My Dad died out of the blue when I was in my mid-twenties; no warning, no time to prepare. When I shared some of this on social media, others told their stories of how rainbows appeared, usually at difficult times, to remind them to hold on to the hope they had in God, that all would work out in the end. In my street, when lockdown started, rainbows began to appear in windows, thanking all the key workers for what they were doing. Mine still hangs in our window.

A rainbow is made out of sunshine and rain. This seems quite apt: the mix of life, both things needed for us to thrive. While I prefer the sunshine, I know my need for water; if I don't drink enough water I don't feel as well. If my garden doesn't get adequate water then plants begin to wilt and eventually might die. Rainbows don't appear if there is no rain.

The Christian life is always going to be a mix of experiences. As a teenager, I was very aware that I was called to take up my cross and follow Jesus, and reading the Gospels makes it clear that this is not likely to lead to a happy, pain-free life with no barriers or challenges. But the rainbow is God's promise that even when things go very badly wrong, and that's why we have the story of Noah, there is now a promise between God and God's people and we can hold on to that.

For prayer and reflection

When we see a rainbow, Lord, help us to remember Your promises and fill us with a sense of hope. Amen.

Holy ground

Exodus 3:1–6

'the place where you are standing is holy ground.' (v5)

A place where God speaks may become holy ground to us, as it was for Moses in our passage today. God broke through the natural order and the fire did not consume the bush. There Moses encountered an angel, a messenger of God, and heard God speak to him. This was a place of awe for Moses, something we too can glimpse when we feel we are on holy ground.

What encourages me about this passage is that Moses was going about his daily work when he encountered God. When he woke up it probably seemed like any other day, caring for the sheep. God is to be found in the everyday, perhaps not in such a dramatic way as Moses did in this passage, but God can speak to us as we do the most mundane things. I am always encouraged by the stories of Brother Lawrence who is known for practising the presence of God while he was washing up. Our domestic or work responsibilities can become a place of holy ground as God speaks to us.

Perhaps today you might want to recall some of those places which have been holy ground for you and remember what God said then. Are there words or promises you need to revisit? Might there even be a place to return to? I have two places in particular that are holy ground for me, where God speaks significantly and where I have been able to lament and grieve and have a sense of God receiving my offering – of it being holy ground. Places can be significant to us, we can recall God's words, but we can also have an expectation of meeting with God as we go about our daily lives and having that experience of holy ground, if only for a minute or so.

For prayer and reflection

Father, help us to see You in the everyday and to listen to what You say to us as we stand on holy ground. Amen.

Calming the **storm**

Mark 4:35–41

'Why are you so afraid? Do you still have no faith?' (v40)

I get very seasick and feel queasy way before the winds get anywhere near storm force. There is not a chance I would be sleeping! Given that some of the disciples were fishermen, I might think that they would be used to being out on the water in all conditions. Perhaps these were exceptional that evening.

We have been facing exceptional conditions in recent times, and have perhaps faced fear and prayed for the calming of the storms that were facing us. Jesus said to the storm, 'Quiet! Be still!' I look for that internally in the storms that I face. What we see outside can be a reflection of what we are feeling on the inside and Jesus encourages us not to be afraid.

Yet being fearless might not be helpful either and we need to respect nature, not take unnecessary risks and certainly not put others' lives at risk through foolish actions. The Royal National Lifeboat Institution has as its motto, 'with courage, nothing is impossible', but it must be frustrating to have to go out on a rescue, risking your own life, when people have acted foolishly or irresponsibly. I was on a beach once and hadn't realised how fast the tide came in. One big wave made me realise I needed to move quickly.

This story occurs quite early in Mark's Gospel, as the disciples were still getting to know who Jesus is. We too need to continue to get to know Jesus, to deepen our experience of Him, to understand how He works in our lives and to seek that deep peace, particularly in the storms that inevitably come. We can find calmness on the inside when all around us seems stormy – that is what faith in Jesus can bring.

For prayer and reflection

God who calms the storms, give us a sense of deep inner peace and faith in You. Amen.

Consider the **lilies**

I have a small embroidery, completed many years ago, which displays the words, 'consider the lilies'. It comforts me. There is such beauty in nature, such a diversity in flowers, a riot of colour and scent. I try every day to see how God is speaking to me through nature – my spiritual health is enhanced. One walk gives me the opportunity to smell lavender. Another to see trees as they change through the seasons. The grandeur of the poplars gets me looking up at the sky; they help me focus on the bigger picture. When I potter in my garden, I rub the leaves of some of my herbs and take in the variety of scents.

As I have been writing these notes and praying about which passages are most appropriate, I keep returning to these passages of reassurance. Passages that tell us God cares for us, that God will meet our needs. That we need not be afraid. Perhaps the one thing that I take from this passage is the value of being present in the moment, enjoying what is happening now, rather than worrying about what tomorrow will bring. It is something that takes discipline for me, but this passage focuses on two things I can see every day: birds and flowers. So God is giving me reminders every day of His care for me, and there are days when I particularly appreciate this as worries can creep back in. I would love to have a magic wand to banish or change things but my discipleship has not been like that. It has involved daily, sometimes moment by moment, decisions to follow Jesus and trust that this will work out for the good because we have a redemptive God.

Matthew 6:26–34

'not even Solomon in all his splendour was dressed like one of these.' (v29)

For prayer and reflection

Thank You that the God who cares for the birds of the air cares for us too and meets our needs. Amen.

Remembering and storytelling

. . . .

Joshua 4:1–7

'When your children ask in time to come' (v6, NRSVA)

I love what you might call preaching crosses, old stone carved crosses etched with stories from the Bible. They date from a time when people could not read the Bible for themselves. A preacher would tell those stories. I am fascinated by visiting churches and seeing stained glass windows or other things which tell a story. I grew up attending a church dedicated to St Peter so am familiar with those stories because of the images I saw week by week.

We can use objects from nature to tell stories or to mark things. The building of cairns has become much more common; even the local beach we go to on holiday has piles of stones. While it might be a bit of fun, it can also be significant as we remember people or places, or want to leave a marker to recall at a later time.

I love, too, some of the stories associated with natural things, showing how people, as Jesus did, have used what is around them to explain their faith or point to God. What I learnt to call object lessons as a Sunday School teacher has deep biblical roots.

. . . .

Optional further reading

Job 12:7-10; Romans 8:19-22.

Imitating **Jesus**

**Philippians
2:5–11**

'Let the same mind
be in you that was
in Christ Jesus' (v5)

My spiritual health flourishes when my attitudes are in line with those of Jesus. He is the supreme example of how to live our lives. Today's passage is often known as the 'Christ hymn' and may well have been an actual hymn that was sung and then incorporated into the letter to the Philippians.

Sadly, passages like this have been misused at times, encouraging an unquestioning obedience to people who seek to mediate God to us. I am talking here about having an attitude of servant-heartedness, looking at what we can give as well as receive. Looking out for those opportunities that God is calling us to respond to. When we read the Gospels, it is clear that Jesus did not meet every need in His world at that time. He was led by His Father and the Holy Spirit, responding rather than being left burnt out and unable to carry on. That's why imitating Jesus involves taking time out, breaks to pray, refocus, and seeking God.

I wonder what you think is in the mind of Jesus? J.B. Phillips' translation talks of Jesus being the example of what our attitude should be. When I think about this, words like kindness, compassion, encouragement and challenging come to mind. Those are qualities I seek to imitate in Jesus. I find the challenging a little harder sometimes but Jesus challenged the authorities, the injustice He saw; we might do that too. What causes are on your heart? What passions has God given you? What Bible passages resonate and give you a sense of vocation? In what areas of your life do you particularly need to imitate Jesus today?

**For prayer
and reflection**

**Gracious God, we
thank You for the
example we have
in Jesus. Help us
to have that same
attitude. Amen.**

Come and **see**

John 1:35–42

'He went straight
off and found his
own brother,
Simon, and told
him' (v41, Phillips)

Today we celebrate St Andrew, the disciple who, having encountered Jesus, believing him to be the Messiah, went and told his brother Simon, and brought him to meet Jesus. Jesus then renamed Simon, Peter, a rock.

What if Andrew had not responded to the invitation of Jesus to come and see, and then told his brother about him? We will sometimes never know the consequences of seemingly little actions, although clearly Andrew did with this one.

As we finish this month exploring our spiritual health – our relationship with ourselves, others, God and the environment – and as we enter Advent, who might we want to invite to come and see Jesus? People may see Jesus through our words, actions, the way we live our lives. They may encounter Jesus at an event we invite them to or a book we lend or a podcast we suggest. The response to come and see is not our responsibility, it is God's, it is the work of the Holy Spirit. It may feel difficult to be like Andrew and say come and see, but more usually that is part of a wider conversation or journey we have made with friends. Both my husband and I made a commitment to Jesus because of friends who said come and see their church. Our lives are transformed because of it. We both blog regularly, sharing insights, encouragements, questions – another contemporary way of communicating come and see. How might you 'say' come and see today?

What have you seen this month? What are the threads, the thoughts, the actions, the tweaks that you want to make or continue with as this month's journey comes to an end?

**For prayer
and reflection**

Loving God, thank
You for the
example of Andrew.
Help us to
encourage others
to come and see
too. Amen.

One day to **make** a world of difference

GI♥ING TUESDAY

#GivingTuesday 2021

The global day of generosity takes place TODAY
30 November 2021!

Join thousands of people donating to good causes today.

waverleyabbeyresources.org/make-a-donation

Expectation and Wonder

Rosalyn Derges

Revelation 3:20–21

'Here I am! I stand at the door and knock.' (v20)

Throughout December, my husband and I light an Advent candle each evening as we eat supper. And we still like to open the doors on the Advent calendar, especially if they have chocolate inside! The candle and calendar remind us that we are leading up to an event which heralds the arrival of Christmas and, for us, a monumental miracle. This miracle, the coming of God's Son, is certainly something to be celebrated. He came in the flesh as a man, He comes alive in our hearts on a daily basis, and He promises to come in glory at the end of time. How amazing!

Advent is a time for us to reflect on the wonder and joy of it all; a time to prepare our hearts and allow our spirits to be renewed as we bask in the glory of God's precious gift to us in the form of the Christ child. As we begin this journey into Advent, take a moment to quietly consider some of the things in your life that might prevent you from fully embracing the joy of this season. Too many things to do, presents to buy and wrap, food to buy and cook, events to fit in around an already busy schedule. Perhaps we need a new awareness of the coming King; to awaken that sense of anticipation and awe of who our King is and what He has done.

Is it time to open the door of our hearts knowing that our Lord Jesus wants to come in and experience life with us anew in this season of hope and joy to the world? Whether you are one who is weary of this season, or one who fully welcomes it like a wide-eyed child, let's enjoy the journey to Bethlehem and beyond together with expectation and wonder.

For prayer and reflection

Lord, increase in me the joy of Your coming as a baby and each day in my life. May I open the door of my heart to You and experience the wonder of Your presence. Amen.

Become part of someone's testimony

Our Bible reading notes are read by hundreds of thousands of people around the world, and *Every Day with Jesus* and *Inspiring Women Every Day* have recently been made free in the UK. We want everyone, whatever their financial means, to have access to these resources that help them walk each day with our Saviour.

Here's what one Every Day with Jesus reader wrote to us:

Ever since I started using Everyday with Jesus, I reconnected to the Lord directly again. It deals with my day to day and minute to minute problems in details. Guiding me in the most solemn and right direction for a dedicated Christian living.

As we trust in God's provision, we know there are costs to providing this ministry. Do you have a passion for God's Word changing lives? Could supporting this vision be a way in which you serve?

A gift of just £2 a month from you will put daily Bible reading notes into the hands of at least one person who is hungry to know God and experience His presence every day.

Visit **waverleyabbeyresources.org/donate** to become part of someone's testimony, or use the form at the back of these notes.

God's story

**Revelation
1:4–8**

'I am the Alpha
and the Omega,'
says the Lord God,
'who is, and who
was, and who is to
come' (v8)

God's story is quite magnificent, isn't it? If our Advent thoughts just centre around celebrating the birth, we will miss the fullness of that story. It's about His glorious kingdom, creating the earth, encouraging His people to live godly lives, coming to earth as a man to declare who God is, dying as a sacrifice for us to be able to live the abundant love-filled lives He wants us to experience, taking us with Him into eternity and coming to reign as the King of kings. What an incredible story that is – and we are part of it!

God's heart for us is to remember, as well as look forward to all the fullness He offers and the anticipation of His return. The fact that Jesus left the glory of heaven and came to earth enables us to see that God loves, forgives and frees us. He is 'the faithful witness' (v5) to all of this. Jesus humbled Himself to serve the humanity He created; the journey He made from heaven to earth was a costly one, He paid a high price and we are the beneficiaries. Can you imagine heaven's perspective on this? Madeleine L'Engle captured it when she wrote: 'Was there a moment, known only to God, when all the stars held their breath, when the galaxies paused in their dance for a fraction of a second, and the Word, who has called it all into being, went with all his love into the womb of a young girl?'*

Let's pause for a few seconds, breathe in this truth, and accept the grace and peace from the One who is, who always was and who is still to come. This is God's heart for us, He has opened the door of His heart so we can receive the inheritance of His kingdom.

**For prayer
and reflection**

**Glorious Lord, this
is one of the joys of
this season, that it
opens my eyes to
begin to see the
bigger picture and
take in the fullness
of all You have
given. Amen.**

*Madeleine L'Engle, 'A sky full of children'. In *Watch for the Light,* a collection of readings for Advent and Christmas (Walden, NY: Plough, 2001)

Be **creative**

'The Word gave life to everything that was created, and his life brought light to everyone'. (v4, NLT)

A s we approach this Christmas, creating an atmosphere of thanksgiving and worship as we meditate on all that the birth of Jesus means to us can be uplifting. We might consider that the world views this season as an opportunity to celebrate excessively: but what if there is an innate longing in each of us to rejoice, to give and receive gifts, as well as enjoy family at this time of year? God wants us to satisfy those longings in the celebration of His Son's birth, to recognise that the desire to embrace the richness of life is found in Him. We read: 'From his abundance we have all received one gracious blessing after another' (v 16, NLT).

Do you remember the sense of anticipation, wonder and fun when you were a child? Have we lost that in the busyness of our own or others' expectations? I can so very easily become disheartened by the preparations, the crowds bustling about, the questions about what to buy so that everyone will be satisfied ¬ so that what is meant to be joyous becomes a drudge! We have made life so complicated, and our demands for a perfect time are high.

When God created the world, we read that He was so pleased with what He had made; it feels like He did it all with a happy heart, enjoying every second. Perhaps, this year, we could approach this time of Advent with a creative spirit like His as we prepare our hearts to celebrate and adore Jesus. To see what we are doing as a blessing to others in the way God has blessed us. In terms of preparation and expectation, my question is: what can I let go of and what can I embrace?

For prayer and reflection

Oh Lord, help me to focus on You this Advent. I pray I will hold the joy of Your coming in my heart as I prepare in the coming weeks. Amen.

Light of the world

······································

John 8:12; Matthew 5:14

'I am the light of the world. Whoever follows me will never walk in darkness, but will have the light of life.' (John 8:12)

Each weekend we will consider some of the descriptions Jesus used of Himself. Here He declares He is 'the light of the world'. Light brings clarity and perspective; we can see more easily what is ahead and are less likely to trip up. I enjoy many forms of light: candlelight is soft and glowing; firelight is warm and welcoming; streetlights help me to make sense of the road and torchlight on a walk in the dark can be fun.

And what of Jesus' light? It draws us to the fact that He was real and genuine. Light reveals what the darkness hides – and there was nothing hidden where Jesus was concerned. He clearly revealed the truth in everything He did and was. His life was illuminated by His love and excellent character; His passion for being obedient to the Father; and His focus on His purpose to redeem humankind and give us abundant life for all eternity.

The incredible thing is Jesus also calls us the light of the world (Matt. 5:14). We, too, are called to be genuine, real and of good character. When we follow in His light, we step out of the darkness and into His mercy (1 Pet. 2:9-10).

······························

Optional journalling

Write your thoughts down; perhaps make it a prayer.

God has **promised**

Isaiah 9:2–6

'For to us a child is
born, to us a son is
given, and the
government will
be on his
shoulders.' (v6)

Has anyone ever made you a promise that they
reneged on? Or have you promised something
you fully intended to see through, only to
find that you couldn't? Empty promises can be hard to
cope with, can't they? Then there are the promises that
certain things will make us look better, feel better and
achieve more. Those can be empty too. Perhaps we may
even look at some of God's promises and wonder if He
will actually come through for us. We may doubt either
Him or that we are good enough to receive from Him. But
the promises He made concerning the coming of His Son
have been utterly fulfilled, in every way.

What is the promised 'son' going to be like? He will
be like a 'light', people will 'rejoice' because of Him,
He will 'break the yoke of... slavery' (NLT), and come
against those who bring tyranny. The Jewish people
were promised a Messiah who would lead them out of
darkness, slavery and oppression; their expectation
was for a mighty warrior. For some of us, provocation
may come through the behaviour of others; but, for all
of us, freedom comes through the saving power of the
Messiah. The freedom this Messiah brings is connected
to the depth of our inner being. It is our spirit that needs
this Saviour's touch of love and power.

He is our 'Wonderful Counsellor', someone who will
listen and spend time with us. He is a 'Mighty God' who
is powerful and fights for us every moment of every day.
He is an 'Everlasting Father' with a heart towards His
children. He is the 'Prince of Peace' who has given us the
gift of peace. Let's explore those promises and how this
Messiah has fulfilled them.

**For prayer
and reflection**

Precious Jesus,
You are the
promise I need in
my life. You bring
freedom to my
spirit and my soul.
This promise keeps
on giving. Thank
You, Lord. Amen.

Wonderful Counsellor

John 21:12–17

'Lord, you know all things; you know that I love you.' (v17)

The disciples had just been out fishing, trying to return to some semblance of normality after Jesus' death. Peter had been distressed after he had denied knowing Jesus as the trial was taking place. Perhaps this heaviness was still very much with him even though He had seen Jesus after the resurrection. This can happen to us, can't it? We do or say something we're not proud of and can churn it over until it becomes like a thorn pricking our minds on a regular basis.

Sometimes, our way of dealing with it can be to get busy so we can concentrate on something else. Peter was no different. Fishing was the answer; let's get busy! Jesus was on the shore as they found they had nothing in their nets. Advising them to fish in a different direction, they caught a haul that was difficult to bring in. Jesus cooked breakfast and then had this talk with Peter, challenging him about His love. Three times He asked Peter if he loved Him, and three times Peter said of course he did. He was hurt after the third time, but Jesus was doing something deep here. He was gradually releasing Peter from the self-inflicted pain he was enduring. Peter was going to be involved in the birth of God's Church and needed to be liberated from anything that would hold him back. Jesus was being a 'Wonderful Counsellor'. First, He filled the emptiness of Peter's loss as He filled those nets; then, He supplied Peter's physical needs with the breakfast; finally, He showed forgiveness for every denial. What a beautiful way to heal a deep need. This Wonderful Counsellor will do that for us too, and that's a promise fulfilled.

For prayer and reflection

Spend time in Jesus' presence. Let His love and kindness touch you deep within. Bring your needs to Him and let Him fill you, feed you and release you.

Mighty God

Psalm 138

'May they sing of the ways of the LORD, for the glory of the LORD is great.' (v5)

Each new year I choose a verse to help me grow in faith and experience more of Jesus. This year it has been the whole of Psalm 138 as it holds so much of what I need and who God is. This psalm tells us that the promises of God are backed by the honour of His name (v2). This means He must keep His promises and His power is at work in our lives and we can depend on that. There are two important aspects of who He is for me: His majesty and His compassion. These two characteristics are clearly seen in verse 6, 'Though the LORD is exalted, he looks kindly on the lowly'. This mighty God is fully aware of you and me and loves us extravagantly.

We also see that, though we may have trouble in our lives, He will protect us and reach out His hand towards us. The part of our lives He protects is our spirit, our hearts and our minds. In all His interaction with people on earth, His greatest concern was for their inner wellbeing. We cannot control circumstances or what people do, but we can depend on Him to help us deal with how we respond. Jesus said that there would be trouble in this world but that He had 'overcome the world' (John 16:33).

At the end of this psalm we see that the Lord will look out for us and work out His plans for our lives. He created us to have a purpose in His kingdom and He wants us to fulfil that purpose. He has invested His love and power in us through the birth, death and resurrection of Jesus. His promise is that we are His masterpieces created to do good things (Eph. 2:10, NLT). Our 'Mighty God' promises that He will enable us.

For prayer and reflection

Father, You are the 'Mighty God'. Help me to trust You more, depend on You in new ways and understand that Your power is at work in me for good. Amen.

Everlasting Father

'Trust in the
LORD for ever, for
the LORD, the
LORD himself, is
the Rock eternal.'
(Isa. 26:4)

O ne of Jesus' purposes on earth was to display the love, compassion and commitment of His Father towards His children. When we look at Jesus, we can see the Father. The extra dimension we have with *this* Father is that He and His love is eternal, and our hope is that we will be with Him for ever. As the 'Everlasting Father', we have that relationship on earth and in heaven – endlessly! Not only that, but, as the 'Rock', we are also promised that this enduring relationship is safe and secure where we can experience confidence that He will never let us down. And we need that, don't we? Isaiah 54:10 assures us that: 'Though the mountains be shaken and the hills be removed, yet my unfailing love for you will not be shaken'. What a powerful promise.

As Jesus spent His last days with His disciples, He made them this promise we find in John 14, where He tells them He is going to prepare a place for them to live with Him in His Father's house. The beautiful bond Jesus has with His Father is for us to share in as well. We have a part in this, not because of who we are, but because of who He is and what He has done for us. His birth, death and resurrection enable us to enter into that relationship when we open our hearts to this incredible eternal love.

To know we are loved is an absolutely crucial need in our lives. To know we are loved by the King of kings and Lord of lords enables us to live from a place of assurance, acceptance and security. Placing ourselves on the Rock of our salvation, in the arms of the Father and in the heart of Jesus enables us to know we are the beloved child of God.

**For prayer
and reflection**

**Oh Lord, thank You
that You love me
with an everlasting
love. May I place
my life on the Rock
so I may grow in
confidence in my
relationship with
You. Amen.**

Prince of Peace

John 14:25–27; Philippians 4:6–7

'Peace I leave with you; my peace I give you.' (John 14:27)

Many of the Christmas cards we receive this year will probably have a message of peace on them. Jesus must have felt this was an important message too as He spoke encouragement to His friends. There are four aspects to what Jesus says in verse 27. First, peace is a gift. If peace is a gift, we need to receive it and accept it. And as it's a gift from Jesus, we need to expect it to be perfect, that it works, that it will be full-on and not stingy! Second, peace is experienced in our minds and hearts so our thinking and emotions don't have to run riot with anxiety and negativity. Third, the peace Jesus gives is nothing like anything we can get from the world. Accumulating things, adulation from others, circumstances that go our way are great, but they cannot fully satisfy the need for that harmony within our souls that enables us to breathe and be still. Fourth, Jesus says that with His peace we don't need to be troubled, disturbed, worried or afraid. The opposite of being afraid is being brave, courageous and plucky! The opposite of troubled is being calm, easy and composed.

'That's all very well,' I hear you say, 'You don't have my life!' The point is, the peace Jesus gives is not dependent on our circumstances being exactly right, or our relationships being perfect. Jesus' peace is something that dwells deep within us and can rise up when we are knocked, disappointed or hurt. When we have Jesus in our lives, He brings peace with Him. He *is* peace. What a gift! Receive it this Advent. Choose to walk with Him, the 'Prince of Peace'. Let *His* peace fill your heart and your mind.

For prayer and reflection

Reflect on this promise of peace. Receive it, accept it, and let it fill you. Meditate on these verses and choose peace this Advent.

Weekend

The way

....

John 14:4–14

'I am the way and the truth and the life.' (v6)

When God revealed the promise of His Son to Isaiah, we sense that His heart was full of pride for this life-changing arrival that was to come. His descriptions of Jesus were powerful and full of promise. As a Father, He made known His joy at Jesus' baptism when He said, 'This is my Son, whom I love; with him I am well pleased.' (Matt. 3:17). Jesus took on the mantle of those images, not in arrogance, but in humble acceptance of His ministry on earth. He knew the importance of His names and His purpose, one of which was to declare He was 'the way'.

Jesus wants us to know that not only is He the way, but that we can trust Him because He is also truth. Truth is related to promises; we can believe what He says and depend on it. He adds that He is the life, that His life is beating within us. Three influential aspects to fill us with confidence. When we read this, we can also declare, 'You lead me in the way I should go, You always reveal the truth and You give me life. Thank You, Lord.'

Reflect on Jesus as the way and consider how He may be leading you.

....

Optional further reading

Psalm 32:8; 37:4–7; Isaiah 30:18,21; 48:16–17

Hope of the world

'Here is my servant,
whom I uphold,
my chosen one in
whom I delight'
(v1)

How do you prepare for this season of Christmas? We may try to get ahead as far as is possible, so we are free to enjoy the days of celebration. Being someone who prefers to be prepared, I actually *need* to do this! These verses in Isaiah show that God has, and always has had, a plan. His vision is far beyond ours and stretches way into eternity. We cannot comprehend it fully but we can trust it. The Father's revelation of the hope that the coming Saviour would bring raises an expectation of someone who would come with justice and freedom. He also reveals something of the character of Jesus here which tells us that He will be a mighty leader with a tender heart.

He will not be loud or forceful. His gentleness brings kindness to those who are broken or fragile. Justice is where He sets His face; He will be determined to see it done. He will show people the way of truth, to help them see where they may have been confused. He will bring freedom to those who are in darkness, feeling depressed and imprisoned by things that have hurt them. God knows we get burdened by life and what it sometimes throws at us. He understands we need the kind of help that will bring us hope. As we reflect on this description of the promised Saviour who will become our hope, may we experience a healing from our pain, a light in our darkness and wisdom for our way forward.

Jesus is fully prepared. He knows who you are, what you need and how to help you. His kindness and understanding are all you need to experience a release from your 'prison'. He is your hope, your light and your salvation. Always.

For prayer and reflection

Hope of the world, as You step into my life, bring me hope, kindness, healing from hurts. Thank You that You understand and know me. Amen.

Develop your leadership in public service

A brand new MA in Public Leadership begins at Waverley Abbey College in January 2022.

Over 7 modules, students on this innovative course will consider the role of faith in the public sphere and how faith integrates with leadership.

Do you work in the sphere of public leadership? Perhaps you're in healthcare, education, government, politics or the charity sector. If you're interested in developing your leadership potential and understanding how your faith can be used as a force for positive change, then this course is for you.

As a part-time, distance-learning course over three-years, you'll be able to fit in study around your work commitments.

To find out more and apply, visit
waverleyabbeycollege.ac.uk

Or join us for an Open Day in November. Sign up on
waverleyabbeycollege.ac.uk/open-days

Invest in your mental health and wellbeing

Our online courses provide you with the knowledge and skills to understand mental health issues that some people struggle with. Whether you're finding out more by yourself, or journeying together with a group, you'll discover insights into mental health and wellbeing. You'll learn how to navigate challenges yourself or support other people.

Courses currently available from Waverley LEARN

An Insight into Anxiety

An Insight into Self-Esteem

**Paraclesis:
A series on pastoral care**

They're all available for you online at a price of £25 each.

To find out more and to buy a course, visit

waverleyabbeyresources.org/online-courses

Waiting **hopefully**

Luke 2:25–35

'I have seen your salvation, which you have prepared for all people.' (v30, NLT)

Because of the promises Simeon would have known from the Scriptures, he was waiting with anticipation for the coming of the Lord. God made him an exceptional promise that he would not die until he had seen the Messiah. We can learn much from Simeon's attitude and character as he waited. He was righteous and devout, showing he had a true assurance of who God is and how that relationship influenced his life. Simeon was waiting with a sense of hope and expectation that God would fulfil His promises. Waiting is something we are not always keen to do is it? Yet waiting with a sense of hope and knowledge that God is faithful shows a wisdom that will grow and deepen as we depend on Him and get to know Him.

The Holy Spirit was on Simeon, he was tuned into what God was doing. Being assured of the promise God made him shows a confidence in and an intimacy with God. Simeon had a focus on and an awareness of spiritual matters relating to God's kingdom which enabled him to experience clear direction. The Spirit led him to the Temple at just the right time and he recognised the significance of this baby. I suspect his heart was so full of wonder at this point that he just could not help but gather Jesus up in his arms and praise his Father for this miraculous encounter. The promise he had been given was fulfilled.

As we encounter God in our devotional times, do we expect to hear from Him? Can we wait with eager anticipation in His presence? Do we open ourselves to the leading of the Holy Spirit? Might we gather Jesus up in our hearts and worship Him? May we prepare our hearts like Simeon to receive.

For prayer and reflection

Reflect on what waiting in God's presence looks like for you. Ask Him to increase your confidence in how He wants to communicate with you.

Joy

Anna was in the Temple at the same time as Simeon and saw him talking with Mary and Joseph. Anna was widowed at a young age and subsequently gave her life to worshipping in the Temple. She positioned herself there as an act of devotion to God. It was, for her, where God dwelt. Where do we position ourselves? Where are we in relation to God's indwelling? We are unlikely to spend days and nights inside a place of worship as God has clearly told us He dwells with us wherever we are. We have right standing with God because of His grace through Jesus, which results in eternal life and always being in His presence. We are, like Anna, in that place day and night because He never leaves us.

Perhaps we should pause and consider the significance of that truth. When we take hold of this and stand on it, the possibilities of us being able to tune into God's heart and purpose for us increase. It will enable us to become more aware of what He is doing around us so that we can take part in His kingdom purposes, as Anna did. She instinctively knew who this child was and began to share her joy — she could not contain it!

So what does Anna show us in these two verses? She experienced the presence of God in her life so she knew Jesus when she saw Him, and she broke out in praise as a response. How do we respond to the presence of Jesus? Remembering His birth, why He came and the promise His life holds for us can be such a joy for us this Advent. Both Simeon and Anna were deliberate in their expectation of God's presence. They sought Him out, gave time to devotion and received incredible joy. So can we.

Luke 2:36–38; Romans 5:21

'She gave thanks to God and spoke about the child' (Luke 2:38)

For prayer and reflection

Heavenly Father, Your presence is always with me. Help me to become more aware of and receive that truth in my life as I worship You. Fill me with Your joy. Amen.

His presence **changes** things

Luke 2:34–35;
Colossians
1:3–6

'It is bearing fruit
everywhere by
changing lives, just
as it changed your
lives' (Col. 1:6,
NLT)

A new baby changes life; they bring a new dynamic to the home and relationships. This baby was destined to bring transformation. Mary's life had already changed dramatically, but I wonder what she felt when Simeon turned to her with the words, 'And a sword will pierce your own soul too.' (Luke 2:35) It's not something a young mother wants to hear. But this child would grow to be man who would change the world, and Simeon recognised the agony Mary would face. I wonder, too, if these words came flooding back to her as He hung on the cross years later. One wouldn't forget words like that.

What influence does Jesus have in our lives? What change does He bring? He inspires and shapes our behaviour, perceptions, goals, focus, and even relationships. Nothing is ever the same again. When we truly let Jesus into our lives, His love transforms us and our goal is to become more like Him. As a young child in a Sunday School class, I heard the story of Jesus welcoming children and not turning them away. The picture we were shown was of a happy, smiling man with loving, welcoming eyes. I was hooked in that moment and love grew in my heart for Him. That love has consistently influenced my life. Paul wrote this letter to the Colossians when he was under house arrest in Rome. His love for the church at Colosse and the concern for the challenges they faced caused him to write this letter of encouragement, despite his circumstances. His life was spectacularly transformed when he encountered Jesus and his heart was changed towards the Lord, others and himself.

**For prayer
and reflection**

**Today we can ask
ourselves, 'How
does the presence
of Jesus influence
my life?' and 'What
would I like to see
change currently?'**

Expectation

W e said, at the beginning of this devotional, that Advent is a time of preparing our hearts for the coming of the King. We have seen that Simeon was filled with the Spirit in preparation for receiving his promise, and Anna positioned herself in the Temple as a worshipper. What is our expectation? How might we prepare our hearts to experience a deeper encounter with our Saviour? First, we need to recognise the value of what we read here, that our bodies are temples of the Holy Spirit, a place where Jesus wants to dwell. Isn't that wonderful? Advent can be a time where we prepare that temple and focus on His indwelling.

Second, we may need to do a bit of tidying up to get our hearts ready! Talking to Jesus about the things that concern us brings light into some of those dusty corners. Confessing the issues that play on our minds or things we are not so proud of will clear the ground of debris. Letting His Spirit breathe life into our spirit will fill our hearts with a freshness, bringing joy and peace. When we open ourselves to the work of the Spirit in this temple of ours, we can expect so many things. Knowing that we are lavishly loved, we can expect to feel secure in Him. Knowing this Christ child grew to be a man who sacrificed Himself for us, we can expect to feel valued. When the Spirit is living within us, we can expect to be guided and shown the way to fulfil our God-given abilities.

I have heard it said that if you expect little you will not be disappointed. With Jesus and His Spirit living in us, we can expect great things. Do not settle for less, settle for more!

---

1 Corinthians 6:19–20; John 14:15–17

'Do you not know that your bodies are temples of the Holy Spirit' (1 Cor. 6:19)

For prayer and reflection

Precious Jesus, wonderful Holy Spirit, thank You for coming to live in my life. Help me to expect to see You work within me so I can expect more. It's all about You. Amen.

Weekend

Jesus is personal

....

John 14:10–21

'On that day you will realise that I am in my Father, and you are in me, and I am in you.' (v20)

Jesus said 'I am in my Father' many times, declaring the intimacy of the relationship between them. The incredible thing is, we have been included in that cherished relationship. These encouraging words of Jesus reveal that the Holy Spirit is in us also as a counsellor, bringing truth and guidance. There is such power in this connection with the Trinity, along with devotion and support. Jesus clearly wants us to be part of this union pulsing with extravagant life.

This week we have focused on the concept of expectation and have asked questions about how we respond to the changes Jesus brings into our lives. As we see His heart towards His Father and ourselves, might we be drawn into that intimacy so we can make some 'I am' statements of our own: 'I am in Jesus and He is in me', 'I am cherished by the Father and I cherish Him', 'I am filled with the Spirit and respond to His truth'. This love we have with Him empowers us to walk in obedience, which is our loving response to the King who has sacrificed so much out of love for us.

....

Optional further reading

Jesus' prayer for us in John 17:20–26

Angels

'I am Gabriel. I stand in the presence of God, and I have been sent to speak to you' (v19)

H ave you ever considered the role of the angels during Advent and the birth of Jesus? They brought the good news of God's plan and purpose to individuals who became part of this wonderful story. God, over the years, has chosen angels to deliver many messages to His people. And we can sense the excitement of heaven as these angelic beings brought this particular news.

Early in Matthew and Luke, we read about many visits from angels; they knew the news they brought was ultimately life-changing. Here, Gabriel visits Zechariah, revealing he would father a son even though he was an old man. He visited Mary with news that she would have a baby by the power of the Holy Spirit (Luke 1:26–38). An angel revealed God's purposes to Joseph in a dream, so he would understand the value of his role in the birth of the Messiah (Matt. 1:20–25). Angels visited shepherds on the hillside to announce the birth of the Saviour, and then worshipped, glorifying God (Luke 2:8–15). The ministry of the angels here was to inform people of God's plan and to bring Him glory.

Zechariah's response was disbelief at first, and it was here Gabriel revealed the importance and gravity of his news. Gabriel boldly announced who he was: 'I am Gabriel. I stand in the presence of God'. What he said held authority. Yet, when John was born, Zechariah acknowledged God's hand in this and prophesied with heartfelt praise (Luke 1:68–79). I wonder if, as we reflect on the angels, we might get a glimpse of the role that the whole of heaven had as God's Son was born, and that the glory of God was unveiled by how the news was delivered?

For prayer and reflection

Lord God, as I reflect on the angels bringing both good news and glory to You, fill my heart with wonder at this amazing story of the Saviour of the world. Amen.

Elizabeth

Luke 1:5–7,24–25,39–45

'But why am I so favoured, that the mother of my Lord should come to me?' (v43)

I n the culture of the time, childlessness was not only a disappointment but also seen as a disgrace, even as a sign of God's judgment. Yet Luke described Elizabeth as 'righteous' and blameless (v6). Her faithfulness was not diminished because of her status. Perhaps she leaned into God more fully, trusting in Him. My story is a little like Elizabeth's, waiting for years to have a family without success. My route was adoption which, for me, was the most wonderful experience. The agony of the wait, though, can be very painful and you question why. But trusting in God's faithfulness and His plan for your life is definitely something to focus on as a comfort to the soul. We can often see God's life-enhancing plan for us with hindsight, how He works out His purposes through us. Elizabeth's son was going to be no ordinary child, and she was overjoyed to know God was in this (v25).

The beauty and spiritual maturity of Elizabeth is really seen in her response as Mary comes to visit her. First, at Mary's greeting, the baby within her leaped and she was filled with the Holy Spirit. Then, she exclaimed an acknowledgement of the fact that Mary carried the child who would be her Lord. She knew in her spirit who He was. Her next thought was that she was privileged to have a visit from Mary as the 'mother of my Lord'. Finally, she affirmed Mary since she had believed and accepted what God had told her. What a beautiful greeting. Her affirmation must have been such a comfort to Mary who may well have experienced the opposite of that from others. What a fantastic friend and supportive relative to have!

For prayer and reflection

Consider the character of Elizabeth – her humility, encouragement, her awareness, her spiritual understanding.

Mary

'Greetings, you who are highly favoured! The Lord is with you.' (v28)

I find this one of the most breathtaking stories of Advent! We have read that Gabriel stood in the presence of God, a powerful being who was entrusted with the news of God's incredible plan. His dignity and bearing would have been impressive. Mary was 'greatly troubled' at this greeting, and Gabriel seeks to reassure her by saying she has found favour with God and that God is with her. She has been chosen for the highest honour a woman has ever had. The angel explains what this mighty plan is for her, and who she is to give birth to. He will be called Jesus, He will be great, the Son of God, He will sit on a throne, He will reign over Israel and His kingdom will last for ever. What a promise! And not one that would be easily taken in.

What happens next is surprising. She responds with a question. I sense that Mary has an inner strength here; in spite of being in the overwhelming presence of an angel, and the astounding news he brings, she has the courage to ask him how it is going to happen. The miraculous event that will take place comes from the Holy Spirit, as with God nothing is impossible. Her response is, again, full of courage and obedience: 'May it be to me as you have said'. Mary is fully open to God leading her into His kingdom purposes. What trust. We are also chosen women of God; He has a role for us in His kingdom too. When we look to Him and are open to His leading, trusting in the promises in His Word, we too can birth something remarkable and life-changing. Mary's simple faith and glorious attitude can encourage us to ask the Lord to lead us into all He has for us.

For prayer and reflection

Mighty God, nothing is impossible for You. May my attitude be like Mary's, who trusted and obeyed You, co-operating with Your Spirit. Show me Your way, Lord. Amen.

Mary's **song**

Luke 1:46–55

'My soul glorifies the Lord and my spirit rejoices in God my Saviour.' (vv 46-7)

A fter Mary's visit from Gabriel, she hurried to see Elizabeth. Elizabeth's unexpected news must have thrilled Mary and she would have wanted to support her. When Mary visited her, the welcome she received and the affirmation she was given compelled her to worship and declare how great God is. This encouragement from Elizabeth was just what was needed to release this song of praise. So often the circumstances we find ourselves in can cause us to be locked up in terms of worship. We can allow the pressures of life to deplete us from expressing our praise to God. A kindly reassurance and inspiration from others can help to release us from holding back.

This beautiful song of praise shows us how clearly Mary understood the position she was in. She acknowledges her humility before a mighty God and then shows she realises that her legacy as the mother of His Son will be known for ever. She declares who God is and what He has done. Mary speaks of His mercy towards those who need Him and understands He values humility. She appreciates that this child she carries will be part of the deliverance of Israel as her Saviour. He is the promise fulfilled.

What an amazing three months these women must have had. Their love for the Lord and each other, their worshipful attitude and Spirit-filled hearts will have created a wonderful atmosphere. May we be part of a community like that where we are free to worship and hear God speak into our situations. May we find women with whom we can share life and see God at work. May we be encouragers who affirm others in their gifts and walk in life.

For prayer and reflection

Lord, may I be an encourager, one who affirms the gifts of others. Lead me into relationships where we thrive and bring glory to You. Amen.

JAN/FEB 2022

January
WALK THIS WAY
JEN BAKER

February
HE'S IN THE WAITING
CLAIRE MUSTERS

In **January**, Jen Baker guides you in studying four ordinary people trusting an extraordinary God. As they risked stepping into unknown territory, so can we as we step into 2022.

In **February**, Claire Musters looks at what biblical characters learned in those 'in between' times, when God didn't move in the way they expected him to. Discover what we can learn from their experiences for our own lives today.

Available in a variety of formats

Joseph

**Matthew
1:18–25**

....

'When Joseph woke
up, he did what the
angel of the Lord
had commanded
him' (v24)

W hen he learned about Mary's pregnancy, Joseph determined to keep it quiet so she would be spared the humiliation and danger of the Law. Joseph was a righteous man (v19), and that statement describes his honour, integrity and willingness to choose what is good. His attitude and behaviour need to be celebrated, as he showed he was also chosen by God as a man He could entrust His Son to. Joseph was also visited by an angel, this time in a dream. He was told not to be fearful of taking Mary as his wife because God was in this. Joseph was also affirmed as a 'son of David'; he would have been familiar with the fact that the Saviour was to come from the line of David (Matt. 1:2–16).

Joseph did not procrastinate about this dream; he did exactly what the angel had commanded. He was obedient to God's call. Later, Joseph responded with action after other angelic visitations in dreams which were strategic in the life of this little family. To protect Jesus from Herod, they fled to Egypt; then he was informed they were free to go back to Israel as it was safe; and finally was directed to go to Nazareth where they took up residence (Matt. 2:13–23). Joseph did not hesitate to follow God's leading, showing he was the kind of father under whose guidance Jesus would thrive and grow up well.

When God calls us to serve Him, He equips us with all that we need to fulfil the promise within us, but character is something that develops over time. As the Spirit takes up residence within us, He creates opportunities for us to mature. Like Joseph, may we make good choices enabling good virtues.

Holy Spirit, as I face circumstances and choices, help me to choose well. Develop within me an integrity and maturity that blesses others and brings glory to God. Amen.

Weekend

The resurrection and the life

....

John 1:1–18; 11:25
'The Word became flesh and made his dwelling among us.' (John 1:14)

This weekend, we enjoy the culmination of all we have prepared for as we celebrate with family and friends. John writes a celebratory declaration of who Jesus is; that He is the Word and came to live with us. Jesus is the light that shines in the darkness, but people did not recognise Him; yet for those who did, He gave the right to be called 'children of God'. John speaks out about His grace and truth, and that we are the recipients of one blessing after another.

Back in Bethlehem, in a manger, a newborn baby was visited by shepherds because angels had come to them too. It was a humble beginning for one who had created the world and would rule it with authority. The man described in John 1 began life in lowly conditions but would be lifted up and seated in heavenly places and reign over all the heavens and earth. Jesus referred to Himself as 'the resurrection and the life', which means we get to live eternally too. This Christmas weekend, celebrate Jesus as the newborn King, as the living Word, as the way to the Father and as the resurrection and the life.

....
Optional further reading

Reflect on the words of the carol *Hark the Herald Angels Sing*

The **wonder**

'Great is the LORD and most worthy of praise; his greatness no one can fathom.' (v3)

We began this devotional by considering that the Christmas story is part of a magnificent plan that began with creation and runs through God's commitment to and love of His children. It involves the birth, life, death and resurrection of His Son and continues through the work of His Spirit in our lives, now and in the future. The question is, do we still wonder at it all? Can we still stand in awe of the God who is great and worthy of praise? As we move towards the end of this year and look into the eyes of the next, can we take a few moments this week to consider the wonder of who God is and appreciate the good things He has done?

This is a beautiful psalm of praise where King David declares how full of wonder he is at who God is. David did not have the benefit of knowing Jesus and seeing how His life reflected the kindness and Father heart of God, and yet he understood the fulness of the character of God. Here, David speaks about God's greatness, His mighty works, the splendour of His majesty and His power. He worships Him for His abundant goodness and sings of His righteousness. Praising God for who He is takes our eyes off ourselves and focuses them on the joy of God's glory. When we do that, it does something for us too; it reframes how we see our lives and enables us to appreciate our relationship with the creator of our own life. David, like us, faced challenges, behaved in ways that were less than righteous, didn't always walk in obedience, yet he knew that when he praised God his spirits lifted as he focused on his life-giver. Praise stirs up wonder and appreciation in us.

For prayer and reflection

May I encourage you to use this psalm as a prayer of praise? As you pray it out begin to sense the wonder of who God is and let that wonder fill your spirit with worship.

Who is God?

Considering the wonder of who God is, we find a number of attributes that will fuel our time of praise in these verses. He is gracious and compassionate, slow to anger and rich in love, He is good, trustworthy, faithful and righteous. Wow! This is our Father. He has everything a woman needs to feel cherished and special. God knows we need it — He made us, after all. Letting these qualities of a loving Father touch our hearts brings joy to our inner being that affects how we live out our lives each day.

David also reminds us of some of the things this loving Father does to show how much He cares. He lifts up those who are feeling low, He satisfies our desires, He is close to us as we come to Him, He hears our cries and helps us. We can feel confident coming to Him with what's on our hearts because He wants to bless us. Gratitude for who God is and what He has done is a route to experiencing His presence. He is always with us, but how aware are we of this? Do we wake up with a sense of God's presence with us? Proverbs 8:34 in *The Message* says, 'Blessed [is] the woman, who listens to me, awake and ready for me each morning, alert and responsive as I start my day's work'. The awesome truth is that God is at work all around us and wants to join in with that kingdom work.

Mary and Joseph, Elizabeth and Zachariah joined in, Anna and Simeon were prepared each day, the angels obeyed the call to declare the coming of Jesus and the shepherds ran to tell everyone they met. We will join a host of those who were filled with reverence for the God who called them into His amazing story.

Psalm 145:8–21

'The LORD is gracious and compassionate' (v8)

For prayer and reflection

Gracious Father, I praise You for Your love and faithfulness. Thank You that I can trust You to care for me. Help me to be more aware of Your presence each day. Amen.

Holiness

**Luke 1:35;
Psalm 29:1–4**

'Worship the
LORD in the
splendour of his
holiness.' (Psa.
29:2)

God is holy, it is who He is. We stand in awe and wonder at His glory and magnificence. When Gabriel visited Mary, he said, 'the holy one to be born will be called the Son of God' (Luke 1:35). Yet all this holiness and magnificence was set aside so that the Son of God would become a tiny, dependent and vulnerable baby. That in itself should take our breath away. Jesus, in His holiness, showed the most incredible love by becoming one of us, which has enabled us to understand something of who we worship and why. In Psalm 29, David expressed his awe and wonder at the Lord who is powerful and mighty; in Luke we see how we can worship the God who became personal and sacrificed Himself for us.

How do you envisage God's holiness? I sometimes sense it in times of sung worship when we are utterly lost in wonder, love and praise. I feel it in times of personal prayer when I envisage His throne, or when I see a beautiful sun setting over the ocean. God reveals His holiness in ways that create that sense of reverence within us. As His daughters, we too have been called to holiness. God has created us in His image and so we can reflect that part of His nature. It is as we consider who He is, rejoice in the Son, and let His Spirit live within us that we can grow in this attribute. Ephesians 1:4 tells us that we have been chosen 'to be holy'. Can we embrace this in Christ Jesus? May we take on this attitude as we worship Him in the splendour of His holiness? Because of Jesus, we can. God's holiness is both beautifully intimate and magnificently powerful. Let it fill you with awe and wonder.

**For prayer
and reflection**

**My soul magnifies
the Lord for His
holiness. My soul
is blessed by His
beauty and love.
My soul is
refreshed in His
presence. Holy,
holy, holy are You,
Lord. Amen.**

His divine **power**

'His divine power
has given us
everything we
need for a godly
life' (v3)

Have you ever created a word picture of the characteristics of God? I have often done so with a small group, as it's so good to focus on who He is. After we have created our 'picture', we then underline all the attributes we share with Him as image bearers. Then we consider how that knowledge affects us, and express our thanks. Often, we have stopped to think about which areas we would like to see develop more fully in our own lives so we become mature in Him. These words from Peter are such an encouragement as they point us to the fact that we can 'participate in the divine nature' and become more like Jesus. We read that Jesus 'grew in wisdom and stature' (Luke 2:52) — and so can we. Peter goes on to cheer us towards being intentional in that growth by adding these qualities to our lives in increasing measure, which will lead us to being effective and productive.

As we have been considering who God is this week, has there been an area of growth you would like to see develop in your own life? What about the ones we read today? Goodness (good character), knowledge (spiritual understanding), self-control (awareness of personal discipline), perseverance (patient endurance), godliness (reverent wonder), brotherly (sisterly) kindness (warm affection), and love. There is a richness about living this way. It brings us peace in our hearts as our attitudes towards others grow in grace. There is also a sense that we will feel more at ease within ourselves and our relationship with God. Jesus' life was lived and given for us so we could have life in all its fulness. Let's live it well.

For prayer and reflection

Create a 'word picture' of God's characteristics. Underline the ones we can reflect. Ponder on which one or ones you would like to see develop in your own life.

Be **rooted**

'Your faith will grow strong in the truth you were taught, and you will overflow with thankfulness.' (v7, NLT)

Often, as we end one year we begin to look towards the next with anticipation. Some things we will want to leave behind and some we will want to take with us. We might ask, what has been significant for me? What do I want to see change in my circumstances or in myself? These are big questions that can be healthy to consider, rather than just shifting from one moment to the next. Having a time of reflection can guide us towards our future with a greater sense of vision and intention. Paul wrote these words to Christians who were faced with others' belief systems that challenged their faith. We also have challenges and distractions that could so easily confuse our intentions to go deeper with God.

Jesus described Himself as 'the vine' (John 15:1–8), where He tells us that we are the branches who are grafted into Him. We get our life and nourishment from being joined with Him. Here, Paul encourages us to continue to live in Christ and to let our spiritual roots grow down into Him and our lives be built on Him. In our desire to grow in strength and wisdom, we need to lean on Jesus, depend on His strength and be filled by the Holy Spirit – we cannot do this alone. We have talked about holiness, growing in the characteristics of God, and becoming more like Jesus, but we aren't perfect and never will be! However, if we choose to set our hearts on accepting Jesus as Lord, follow Him, be rooted in Him, then faith will grow stronger and we will begin to mirror who He is. Jesus came as a baby and grew into a man who reflected the image of His Father. How will we grow in this coming new year?

**For prayer
and reflection**

Father, as I consider this amazing story, thank You that You have made me part of it. Show me how to grow in the richness of Your love, rooted in You. Amen.

Order form

Get Your **FREE** Daily Bible Reading Notes **TODAY!** (UK ONLY)

Your favourite Bible reading notes are now FREE. God has called us back to the original vision of CWR to provide these notes to everyone who needs them, regardless of their circumstance or ability to pay. It is our desire to see these daily Bible reading notes used more widely, to see Christians grow in their relationship with Jesus on a daily basis and to see Him reflected in their everyday living. Clearly there are costs to provide this ministry and we are trusting in God's provision.

Could you be part of this vision? Do you have the desire to see lives transformed through a relationship with Jesus? **A small donation from you of just £2 a month, by direct debit, will make such a difference** Giving hope to someone in desperate need whilst you too grow deeper in your own relationship with Jesus.

4 Easy Ways To Order

1. Visit our online store at **waverleyabbeyresources.org/store**
2. Send this form together with your payment to: **Waverley Abbey Trust, Waverley Abbey House, Waverley Lane, Farnham, Surrey GU9 8EP**
3. Phone in your credit card order: **01252 784700** (Mon–Fri, 9.30am – 4.30pm)
4. Visit a Christian bookshop

For a list of our National Distributors, who supply countries outside the UK, visit waverleyabbeyresources.org/distributors

Your Details (required for orders and donations)

Full Name: ID No. (if known):

Home Address:

                                              Postcode:

Telephone No. (for queries):   Email:

Publications

TITLE	QTY	PRICE	TOTAL
		TOTAL PUBLICATIONS	

UK P&P: up to £24.99 = **£2.99**; £25.00 and over = **FREE**

Elsewhere P&P: up to £10 = **£4.95**; £10.01 – £50 = **£6.95**; £50.01 – £99.99 = **£10**; £100 and over = **£30**

| Total Publications and P&P (please allow 14 days for delivery) | **A** | |

Payment Details

☐ I enclose a cheque made payable to CWR for the amount of: **£** _____

☐ Please charge my credit/debit card.

Cardholder's Name (in BLOCK CAPITALS) _____

Card No. ☐☐☐☐ ☐☐☐☐ ☐☐☐☐ ☐☐☐☐

Expires End ☐☐ ☐☐   Security Code ☐☐☐

Continued overleaf >>

<< See previous page for start of order form

| One off Special Gift to Waverley Abbey Trust | ☐ Please send me an acknowledgement of my gift | B | |

GRAND TOTAL (Total of A & B)

Gift Aid (your home address required, see overleaf)

giftaid it I am a UK taxpayer and want CWR to reclaim the tax on all my donations for the four years prior to this year **and on** all donations I make from the date of this Gift Aid declaration until further notice.*

Taxpayer's Full Name (in BLOCK CAPITALS) _____

Signature _____ **Date** _____

*I am a UK taxpayer and understand that if I pay less Income Tax and/or Capital Gains Tax than the amount of Gift Aid claimed on all my donations in that tax year it is my responsibility to pay any difference.

Your FREE Daily Bible Reading Notes Order

	Please Tick	FREE	£2 pcm	£5 pcm	£10 pcm	Other
Every Day with Jesus		☐	☐	☐	☐	☐ £___
Large Print *Every Day with Jesus*		☐	☐	☐	☐	☐ £___
Inspiring Women Every Day		☐	☐	☐	☐	☐ £___

All CWR Bible reading notes are also available in single issue **ebook** and **email subscription** format. Visit **waverleyabbeyresources.org** for further info.

CWR Instruction to your Bank or Building Society to pay by Direct Debit

Please fill in the form and send to: CWR, Waverley Abbey House, Waverley Lane, Farnham, Surrey GU9 8EP

DIRECT Debit

Name and full postal address of your Bank or Building Society

To: The Manager _____ Bank/Building Society

Address _____

Postcode _____

Name(s) of Account Holder(s)

Branch Sort Code

Bank/Building Society Account Number

Originator's Identification Number

| 4 | 2 | 0 | 4 | 8 | 7 |

Reference

Instruction to your Bank or Building Society

Please pay CWR Direct Debits from the account detailed in this Instruc subject to the safeguards assured by the Direct Debit Guarantee. I understand that this Instruction may remain with CWR and, if so, detai will be passed electronically to my Bank/Building Society.

Signature(s)

Date

Banks and Building Societies may not accept Direct Debit Instructions for some types of account

For a subscription outside of the UK please visit www.waverleyabbeyresources.org where you will find a list of our national distributors.

How would you like to hear from us? We would love to keep you up to date on all aspects of the CWR ministry, including; new publications, events & courses as well as how you can support us.

If you **DO** want to hear from us on email, please tick here [ ] If you **DO NOT** want us to contact you by post, please tick here
You can update your preferences at any time by contacting our customer services team on 01252 784 700. You can view our privacy policy online at waverleyabbeyresources.org